Endorsements

I have known Evonne Boggs for more than two decades. I have a tremendous amount of admiration, respect, and love for her. She has dedicated her life to meeting the needs of others, whether by serving in the military or being a homeland missionary, staff children's minister, church planter, Bible study leader, wife, mother, and grandmother. Her steps align with Christian service and reflect her love for Christ.

Evonne is a mighty woman of prayer. She has a strong commitment to helping women experience the power of prayer. On numerous occasions, I have participated in prayer experiences that Evonne has orchestrated. While each prayer experience has been unique, there remains a common thread throughout, in which Evonne has created an ambiance of reflection, restoration, and rest.

Spiritual Oasis is a written treasure as Evonne shares her vision, creativity, and practical insights to help you discover the transforming power of prayer. If you are seeking simple ways to start a meaningful prayer room in your home, at your church, or for a special event, *Spiritual Oasis* will offer you the inspiration you need to get started today.

—Judy Sansom, Retired Assistant Executive Director, Highland Lakes Camp and Conference Center

Evonne has been a dear friend who I can trust with my prayer needs, and I know that she will continue to pray with me until an answer comes. She has been a great encourager to many, drawing them closer to God through the prayer rooms that she and Paul have set up.

We find in many Bible verses that Jesus often separated Himself to pray. I feel confident that we will all be challenged to find our own quiet place for time alone with God as we read the pages of this book. I can't wait for the blessings ahead! "Pray without ceasing" (1 Thessalonians 5:17 KJV).

—Mary Patton Aquirre, Women's Ministry Leader, Kyle, Texas

Evonne has done a tremendous job planning prayer walks and labyrinths for conferences all over the Texas Hill Country. I've had the blessing of getting to experience many of the labyrinths she has created, and what a worshipful experience! Evonne has a heart for prayer and encourages us through these walks to go humbly and expectantly to our Father.

—Kellee Lemons Parish, Minister of Children and Families, Trinity Baptist Church, Kerrville, Texas

Spiritual

Oasis

Creating a
Getaway
with God in
Your Home

Spiritual
Oasis

Creating a Getaway with God in Your Home

Evonne Boggs

A Worthy Press

Published by A Worthy Press
Chandler, Texas 75758
AWorthyPress.com

Library of Congress Control Number: 2024925121
Paperback: 978-1-956673-85-2
E-book: 978-1-956673-18-0

Cover and Interior Design by PublishandTell.com
Cover photo by

Dedication

This book would have never happened without the help of some special people who God placed in my path.

To Judy Sansom: Thank you for embracing the vision for prayer rooms and giving me the freedom to develop them for so many years at the Highland Lakes Camp and Conference Center women's events. Your trust and support increased my faith in myself and in God's provisions.

To my husband, Paul, who has listened to my visions and made the designs come to life: Thank you for building that whale and for putting a tree inside the prayer room! Your amazing patience and belief in what God was doing through the process made this all possible. You proofread, mentor, construct, and add insights into all aspects of the projects I work on. We are truly a team, and you are a cherished gift from God.

To my daughter, Amy, who is an amazing crafter: When I tell people how talented you are, you always add, "My mom is a talented crafter too." You have made me believe that although our talents are different, they are indeed beautiful and worthy of praise to the Giver. Thank you for believing in me. You are a miracle from God.

Contents

Foreword

This is a powerful, practical short read that could change your life! That's not just a catchy sales line, and Evonne would probably never make such a claim, but I will tell you that what she shares within these pages is that powerful. Why? Because there is power in prayer, and Evonne is here to help us create space for more prayer in our lives.

I first met Evonne at a women's retreat. She had organized a prayer experience, and I was leading a workshop for writers. As we were setting up, we casually said hi across a dusty parking lot. A few moments later, Evonne came into my workshop room and introduced herself. I immediately knew she had a book in her. We connected on many levels, both being military veterans and sharing many other commonalities.

She invited me to visit her prayer room, and so we walked across the dry caliche to a sidewalk that led to a door-sized angel. My intrigue grew. As she opened the angel door and invited me in, tears filled my eyes. Evonne transported me to a Spiritual Oasis! A massive crystal chandelier hung from the center of the room, with white lights billowing out to each corner. The overhead lights were off, drawing attention to the many "stations" around the room, each with its own unique lighting. Like rooms within the room, each station had a different purpose and touched all five senses.

Before even taking a step, I looked at Evonne through my tear-filled eyes and reminded her that she was anointed! I could feel the presence of God in the room. I could also see clearly that Evonne has a gift and is using it! She gave me a brief tour of the setup and then allowed me to experience the room on my own. Later, during the conference, I would come back and take in the *full* experience. I took the time to sit in each space, read the intention, write in my prayer journal, listen, and pray.

Even though each station drew me in, two in particular impacted me in deep ways. In the throne room was a beautiful, oversized armchair fit for a King, with a crown sitting on the seat cushion. I'm tearing up now as I write and remember it. It seemed as though

Jesus had just gotten up from that throne and laid His crown aside to meet me in that space.

The second station felt light and airy—literally! Evonne had set up a fan that blew white gauzy curtains. The backdrop transported visitors to a beach. Like the breeze from the fan, the Holy Spirit was alive and moving in that space!

It had been years since I had visited a prayer room. I realized not only how much I had missed those experiences but also how powerful they are. During that weekend, I invited Evonne to participate in a beach retreat I host for Christian women writers. She marked the dates in her calendar and told me to send her the details. I saw her passion for creating prayer experiences play out as she planned for the beach retreat. We also talked more over the weekend about the books she needed to write, and by the time of the beach retreat, I think I counted at least five.

In a world pulling us in so many directions, we need a place to retreat to. Jesus retreated to the garden to pray, and while I'd love to have a garden, it would need prayer if it were to survive! So I think I'll take the practical advice Evonne gives in this book and create an intentional space in my home.

This concept of a "prayer closet" briefly became popular when it was in a movie some years ago; the focus and features of this "war room" were a bit different than Evonne's Spiritual Oasis, which is personal, artistic, and comfortable. I don't know about you, but the idea of heading to my Spiritual Oasis every day sounds so inviting—knowing God is waiting for me there. I know Evonne says that you can pray anywhere, anytime, but she also says that if Jesus took time away to pray, then so should we.

I pray that through the practicality and inspiration of this book, you'll take action and create this space for yourself. You deserve it ... and you deserve what's waiting for you there.

Publish and tell,

Brenda A. Haire
Heart behind Publish & Tell, Author, and Author Coach

Introduction

P rayer has always fascinated me. When I was young, and someone would announce a "prayer meeting," I wanted to be there. I mean, if anyone was going to spend time meeting with God, I didn't want to be left out! These prayer meetings were times when everyone in the room took turns talking out loud to God. Most people praying sounded so eloquent. I was not one of those. Sometimes I was so shy that no words came out, but what was worse was when a jumble of words rolled out of me like gibberish.

Despite this rocky start, my dedication to prayer remained, and the experiences got better and better as I stepped out in faith.

I joined a national call-in prayer line through the Southern Baptist North American Mission Board (NAMB), and it was then that my commitment to prayer was put to the test. I loved those calls; I kept my Bible in front of me and eagerly answered every new call like it was a divine appointment. My life experiences always seemed to line up with the caller's needs, and God gave me insights I'd never had before.

It was in those times that I connected with prayer in a real way. I began to understand that we all needed God, and our way of accessing Him was by what we call prayer.

Whether we call out to Him alone or with others, the connection to our heavenly Father is the same, and our need to converse with our Creator is a built-in, shared desire. That desire—that calling—is powerful.

I began to design prayer rooms at women's conferences. To some, that means a small room with a lamp, a desk, and a Bible. But to me, it is a place of refuge. In setting up prayer rooms, I wanted to create a beautiful, tangible expression of the prayer focus for each event. The rooms grew from one station to two, to sometimes as many as six, with each station having its own unique design. These spaces helped me and other conference attendees immerse ourselves in the meaning of our prayer time.

Soon, I will write a book about how to set up this type of prayer experience for conferences, churches, and special events. But before I could do that, I felt strongly that I must write *this* book. Prayer begins with us, in our homes. And so, *Spiritual Oasis* was born.

CHAPTER ONE

What Is Prayer and to Whom Do We Pray?

I am so glad you picked up this book! What the world needs most is more believers participating in earnest prayer.

As women, our lives are so busy, and some of us are trying to take care of the whole world. Many of you have a career outside the home; you volunteer for one or more ministries; you care for children (yours and/or someone else's); you have aging parents, a spouse who needs you, your own body that needs attention, a home that needs to be cleaned, meals that must be planned, and—whew! We get tired just thinking about it.

And then we want to squeeze time with God in there somewhere. How do we do it all?

To fit in time for God, we must *begin* with God. Sounds like a no-brainer—something we should have known all along. But life gets busy, and we neglect our relationships, especially the one we need the most.

Your time with God should be an ongoing conversation throughout your day. Let's look at 1 Thessalonians 5:16–18: "Rejoice always, pray constantly, give thanks in everything; for this is God's will for you in Christ Jesus." This is His will for *you.*

From verse 17—"pray constantly"—we learn that you can chat with God as you cook and vacuum and drive the kids to soccer practice. These are casual and simple, ongoing conversations while you are busy with other things because He is with you always. He is a constant life partner.

You may wonder, though, if He wants something more of you. Should your conversation be deeper, more intentional? Let's look at how Jesus prayed. Mark 1:35 says, "Very early in the morning, while it was still dark, he got up, went out, and made his way to a deserted place; and there he was praying." We find this scenario many times in the Bible. The important thing here is not the time of the day but that Jesus "went out ... to a deserted place." We too need a place where we can shut out the busy world and focus on a personal talk with our heavenly Father.

In this book, we will learn how to set aside a place to be alone with God. You can create a place of refuge from the worries of the world—where you can lay them at the feet of Jesus. He is waiting for your loving surrender.

But before we work on our prayer spaces, let's answer the essential question: what is prayer? Essentially, it's a conversation with someone you love. However, this isn't just any *someone*; this is the Creator of the World, the great I AM. Understand His power and His purpose before you come to Him with your requests.

When the Israelites were fleeing Egypt, they ran smack dab into a body of water they could not cross. The enemy was at their back, and before them, certain death by drowning. "But Moses said to the people, 'Don't be afraid. Stand firm and see the Lord's salvation that he will accomplish for you today'" (Exodus 14:13).

What? Stand firm? But, Moses, you don't understand. We are about to die! We hope you are hearing what the Lord said correctly because He is our only hope!

Moses goes on to say, "For the Egyptians you see today, you will never see again. The Lord will fight for you, and you must be quiet" (14:13–14). The New International Version of the Bible says, "You need only to be still."

And so, even in utter panic, they stood still. I can imagine them looking around for a possible escape just in case Moses was mistaken, but no escape was to be found. They held their families close, crying out for mercy, mothers clutching their babies to shield them from the violence of the Egyptians' wrath. *But then God—*

I must quote this passage because it thrills my heart (14:15–22):

> The Lord said to Moses, "Why are you crying out to me? Tell the Israelites to break camp. As for you, lift up your staff, stretch out your hand over the sea, and divide it so that the Israelites can go through the sea on dry ground. As for me, I am going to harden the hearts of the Egyptians so that they will go in after them, and I will receive glory by means of Pharaoh, all his army, and his chariots and horsemen. The Egyptians will know that I am the Lord when I receive glory through Pharaoh, his chariots, and his horsemen."

Then the angel of God, who was going in front of the Israelite forces, moved and went behind them. The pillar of cloud moved from in front of them and stood behind them. It came between the Egyptian and Israelite forces. There was cloud and darkness, it lit up the night, and neither group came near the other all night long.

Then Moses stretched out his hand over the sea. The Lord drove the sea back with a powerful east wind all that night and turned the sea into dry land. So the waters were divided, and the Israelites went through the sea on dry ground, with the waters like a wall to them on their right and their left.

Can you imagine the awe, the fright, and the utter relief as they stepped onto the ground that was just moments ago under water? To the left and the right of them were walls of water, but they traveled safely through on dry ground.

Let's read the rest of the story (14:23–28, emphases mine):

The Egyptians set out in pursuit—all Pharaoh's horses, his chariots, and his horsemen—and went into the sea after them. During the morning watch, the Lord looked down at the Egyptian forces from the pillar of fire and cloud, and threw the Egyptian forces into confusion. **He caused their chariot wheels to swerve and made them drive with difficulty. "Let's get away from Israel," the Egyptians said, "because the Lord is fighting for them against Egypt!"**

Then the Lord said to Moses, "Stretch out your hand over the sea so that the water may come back on the Egyptians, on their chariots and horsemen." So Moses stretched out his hand over the sea, and at daybreak the sea returned to its normal depth. While the Egyptians were trying to escape from it, the Lord threw them into the sea. **The water came back and covered the chariots and horsemen, plus the entire army of Pharaoh that had gone after them into the sea. Not even one of them survived.**

If this seems cruel to you, go back and read the whole book of Exodus. The Israelites were treated harshly as slaves, and Egypt received numerous warnings before this point in the story. The God of the Israelites is not unloving; He is a God of second chances (and many times more).

This, my friends, is the God I pray to. The great I AM is looking out for you. You can trust His Word. You can trust in the Father, Son, and Holy Spirit.

Jesus has full authority as the Son of God. Even the evil spirits know this. Look at this encounter He had with a man possessed by an evil spirit (Mark 5:6–8, emphasis mine):

> When he saw Jesus from a distance, he ran and knelt down before him. And he cried out with a loud voice, "What do you have to do with me, Jesus, **Son of the Most High God**? I beg you before God, don't torment me!" For he had told him, "Come out of the man, you unclean spirit!"

The evil spirit knew Jesus as the Son of the Most High God before others knew it.

And as the Son of the Most High, Jesus has the power to intervene in your life. He can fight your battles and answer your prayers. But you first need to shut out everything else and give Him your full attention.

The power of prayer is in knowing the One to whom we pray and accepting His lordship. You have a part to play here. If you pray without accepting Jesus Christ as your Lord and Savior, it is merely a conversation and not a relationship. You must first:

Acknowledge that you are a sinner. I am not saying you are a bad person. I am only saying that we have all done things that do not honor God and that go against His commands. You must acknowledge that you need His help to not sin.

Believe that Jesus is God's only Son, born of a virgin, crucified on a cross, and risen again on the third day. His blood was the once-and-for-all covering for sins—mine, yours, and all who believe.

Confess your devotion to God the Father, Jesus the Son, and His Holy Spirit with your mouth and believe in your heart.

If the ABCs of salvation are confusing to you or you need further explanation, please go ask someone you trust for more information. I will include the plan of salvation at the end of this book. If you are not a believer, it is not by accident that you are reading this. God is calling you into the family. Don't delay! None of us know how many days we have on this earth. The invitation is open while you are still here.

Have you ever seen a gardener grafting a branch onto a tree or bush? They graft it through a cut. In this process, the two—branch and tree—become one life. This is what we are being told in John 15:5–8 (emphasis mine):

> I am the vine; you are the branches. The one who remains in me and I in him produces much fruit, because you can do nothing without me. If anyone does not remain in me, he is thrown aside like a branch and he withers. They gather them, throw them into the fire, and they are burned. If you remain in me and my words remain in you, **ask whatever you want and it will be done for you**. My Father is glorified by this: that you produce much fruit and prove to be my disciples.

Jesus isn't some ordinary friend. Read John 15:15–17 (emphasis mine):

> I do not call you servants anymore, because a servant doesn't know what his master is doing. I have called you friends, because I have made known to you everything I have heard from my Father. You did not choose me, but **I chose you**. I appointed you to go and produce fruit and that your fruit should remain, so that whatever you ask the Father in my name, he will give you.
>
> This is what I command you: Love one another.

The Son of Almighty God calls you friend. Moreover, you have been grafted into the family of God.

The overall idea of this family relationship is that we will walk with God so closely that whatever we ask will line up with His will for our lives. God is not a magic genie; you will most likely not receive a million dollars on your doorstep or see all your problems disappear. But He hears your prayers. He knows the plans He has for you. He feels your pain. Remember that even though Jesus is divine, He came to earth as fully human and also fully God. He understands pain.

As humans, we have the free will to do whatever we want to do. We mess up. We sin. We can be forgiven, but the consequences of our sins must still be dealt with. The person we hurt may suffer wounds that we cannot heal. Jesus can heal them, but that person has to seek the healing. The drugs a person puts into their body may have lifetime consequences, and some consequences can be passed on to their children. Divorces are broken promises, and the pain and distrust of a broken marriage may last a long time.

Just as what we eat affects our body, so sin affects our lives. A friend's favorite warning on this subject is "We reap what we sow greater than we sow," and I have found this to be true. On the other hand, if you sow faith and love, you will reap an abundance of the same.

We will not always get it right, especially on our own. This is why we need Jesus, and we need to talk to Him: to ask forgiveness, to get guidance, and to give Him gratitude. Thus, prayer.

So what does prayer look like? When I picture it, I see someone talking to their wisest, closest friend. You would come into their presence respectfully because you recognize their position. You come into their presence willingly because you want to be with them in a personal way. You come into their presence as a place of refuge from the noise of the world. You come into their presence with a heart full of thanks.

Prayer really has less to do with your surroundings than it does with the intentions of your heart.

Here are some examples of places where people prayed in the Bible:[1]*

- Samuel cries out to the Lord on the **battlefield** (1 Samuel 7:7–9).

- Nehemiah prays in the king's **palace** (Nehemiah 2:4–5).

- The writer of Lamentations calls on the name of the Lord from a **dungeon** (Lamentations 3:55–57).

- Jonah prays in the **belly of a fish** (Jonah 2:1).

- Jesus prays in the **garden** of Gethsemane (Matthew 26:36).

- Jesus withdraws to the **lonely places** to pray (Luke 5:16).

- Jesus spends the night praying on a **mountain** (Luke 6:12, 9:28).

- A Pharisee and a tax collector go up to the

temple to pray (Luke 18:10).

- Jesus prays on **the cross** (Luke 23:34).

- The disciples pray in an **upper room** (Acts 1:12–14).

- Stephen prays at his **execution** by stoning (Acts 7:59–60).

- Peter retreats to a **rooftop** to pray (Acts 10:9).

- Devout women meet to pray by the side of a **river** (Acts 16:13–14).

- Paul prays with other Christians by the **seashore** (Acts 21:5).

- Paul prays a prayer of thanks on a **ship** during a storm (Acts 27:33–36).

Do you see from these examples that prayer can happen anywhere? Holy ground is any ground where you meet with God.

In Matthew 6:6–13 we are given an example of how to pray:

But when you pray, go into your private room, shut your door, and pray to your Father who is in secret. And your Father who sees in secret will reward you. When you pray, don't babble like the Gentiles, since they imagine they'll be heard for their many words. Don't be like them, because your Father knows the things you need before you ask him.

Therefore, you should pray like this:

Our Father in heaven,
your name be honored as holy.
Your kingdom come.
Your will be done on earth as it is in heaven.
Give us today our daily bread.
And forgive us our debts,
as we also have forgiven our debtors.
And do not bring us into temptation,
but deliver us from the evil one.

Please remember that prayer is a two-way conversation. Be sure to make time to listen for His responses. Having a designated place to pray will help by giving you a place to be quiet and still.

Now that you know what prayer is and the One to whom we pray, are you ready to create your Spiritual Oasis? Come with me, and I'll show you the way...

CHAPTER TWO

Opening Our Home

L et's take a walk into your home and picture it as a visitor would. Invite the Holy Spirit to come in the front door. Take your time as He enters in. What do you see?

By the entrance, you may find keys to your home, vehicles, or storage sheds. A home is a wonderful blessing that not everyone can claim. If you have a home, you are blessed, and that is evidenced by the keys, which represent ownership.

Is there anything in the entrance that tells a visitor that a child of God lives here? If so, imagine how that statement honors the Lord and how it impacts everyone who enters in. On the wall, you may hang a cross or a framed scripture or a picture of God's creation. Well done.

Next, step into your living room or den. This is often the busiest part of the home. It is where we kick off our shoes and relax. There may be a TV or entertainment center. When my kids were little, our living room was often cluttered with toys and books.

This is a place where we can be thankful for those who live in the home with us and whisper prayers of gratitude to God. But it is not usually a good place to be alone with Him. Even when I lived alone, the living room seemed too close to the world I'd just left to find a peaceful prayer space in it.

Now enter your dining room. This is where we share meals. We often pray aloud here. We say blessings over the food God provides and the hands that prepared it.

My children used to do homework at our dining room table, and lots of my unspoken prayers were made there—prayers for patience and wisdom. I wonder now why I didn't verbalize those prayers with my children. I would change that now if I could.

The dining room may also be where you go for family discussions and get-togethers; it would be good to bathe those times in prayer.

Our kitchen is a place where we create meals with loving hands. It can be where we open packages of takeout because the day was just too busy for a home-made meal. That too is a blessing.

Most kitchens represent the woman of the house. I collect teacups, teapots, and salt and pepper shakers that reflect my personality. My kitchen allows you a peek into my quirky nature and personal journey. Like most of you, I like to look out my kitchen window as I prepare meals and wash up. I often talk to God in this space.

Even bathrooms can be places of worship. Bathing my grandchildren and hearing them giggle as we splash bubbles brings back precious memories of when my children were young.

Now with a sister who battles dementia, I am grateful for a tub that she can get in and out of safely when she stays with us. She and I often talk about childhood visits to our grandmother's house, which didn't have indoor plumbing; we had to use an outhouse and bathe in a big metal tub outside. We are so happy to have what we have now!

As you walk through your home, ask God to reveal to you all the blessings you may have been taking for granted as well as all the possibilities in each room. Ask: *Where can I carve out a space to be alone with you, Lord?*

Some thoughts come to my mind:

Closet

Move over, shoes, prayer is coming in! If I'm being honest, some of these can be given to thrift stores that support the homeless or to other local ministries. I have more than I need.

Bedroom

Is there a corner where I can make a space to focus on prayer? I have to be able to face the wall so that my mind won't tell me to lie down on the comfy bed or dust the dresser or pick up the laundry... (See what I mean?)

Guest Bedroom

If you are blessed enough to have an unused bedroom, claim it for prayer. You can always move your prayer to another part of the house when a guest comes. A room divider would be helpful to separate the sleeping side of the room from the praying side.

You could empty the guest room closet and reserve it as a Spiritual Oasis. Attach hooks with hangers on the outside of the closet door if your overnight guests need somewhere to hang their clothes.

Dining Room

If you share this space, you will need your own little corner. Use a room divider or trifold poster board that you can set up when you want to focus on prayer.

Porch

Sitting on my porch brings about prayer effortlessly. As I look over all that God has provided, prayers of thanks fill my mind. I can't look at all He has provided without thinking back to my life before I asked Him to be in it. Profound gratitude fills my heart and spills over into prayer.

If I see people in the distance, my prayers shift to asking God to provide salvation for them as well. *Please, Lord, bring them to Your throne.*

I am also aware that your porch may have lots of distractions. What time of day would be the most peaceful? Pray at that time, and choose the quietest part of your porch. Be mindful of climate control for comfort; I have ceiling fans on my porch that help during our hot Texas summers.

Bathtub

Don't laugh, but I have a saying displayed on the mirror over my tub:

Pray about everything
Worry about nothing

And here I soak and pray. By the time the water gets cold, I have prayed through all my family's needs.

CHAPTER THREE

Ambiance

To begin, ask yourself: *What will my space say about my commitment to prayer? Will it echo my devotion to God? Will the space say, "I have come here to worship God"? Will it say that this is holy ground?*

A place for prayer must also be a place of worship. Declare it as holy ground. When you walk in, envision that you are face to face with Jesus. It is not the actual ground, of course, that is holy; it is the recognition that this place is set aside to meet with a holy God.

Guided by the Holy Spirit, it is here that you will do spiritual warfare with the enemy. That is why some people call it their "war room," which is also the name of the film that Brenda references in the Foreword. As Ephesians 6:12 says, "For our struggle is not against flesh and blood, but against the rulers, against the authorities, against the cosmic powers of this darkness, against evil, spiritual forces in the heavens."

Here, you can reclaim your family, your home, and your situation and declare that God is bigger than all your problems. It is here that you can bow down in the presence of a holy God and ask for His guidance and forgiveness. It is also where you can raise your hands and your voice in loving praise.

When Moses saw the burning bush, the angel of the Lord spoke (Exodus 3:5): "'Do not come closer,' he said. 'Remove the sandals from your feet, for the place where you are standing is holy ground.'" God met Moses there for a specific purpose, and He wanted to be sure that Moses understood the significance of the meeting.

Meeting with God is no ordinary moment. It is not merely something we check off our to-do list. It is an audience with the King of kings, the Lord of lords, the Almighty God, so treat this time and place with awe and respect and loving obedience.

Consider the chorus of the hymn "Holy Ground":[2]

> This is holy ground
> We're standing on holy ground
> For the Lord is present
> And where He is is holy

Whatever space you choose, it must be pleasing to your senses. You can design it in your preferred style with colors that make you feel happy and peaceful. I know a sweet crafter who loves pink and shabby chic. However you design it, it must be meaningful for you. Here are some ideas:

- Shades of blues may remind you of the ocean or the sky.

- Aqua and turquoise give a creative feel.

- Oranges and crimsons look like a majestic sunset.

- Bright orange feels optimistic and enthusiastic.

- Coral can be adventurous. ("Wherever you lead, Lord.")

- Yellow makes a friend of mine feel joyful and alive!

- Reds may make you think of redbirds or the blood of Christ. Red is the color of love and energy.

- Black—yes, even black can be soothing. Some

like it because it is the absence of other things, making the space simple and open to possibility. Its elegance is powerful.

- White stands for purity. It may make you picture a wedding scene.

- Rainbows remind us of the promises of God. A balance of many colors represents harmony and possibilities.

- Pink feels like innocence to me, nurturing and kind.

- Green is a life-giving color. It makes me think of forests and fields. It creates a feeling of life and growth.

- Purple is the color of royalty! I love to use deep purples and gold when I want to convey the feeling of coming before the throne of God.

In addition to colors, lighting is important. You want lighting that is bright enough to read by but gentle enough to soothe.

And don't forget about your comfort level. Is the room too hot or too cold? Comfort is critical. If your legs are cramped or your back hurts, you won't be able to focus long on prayer.

What sounds soothe you? Should you have a playlist on your phone, a sound machine, or a speaker in your room?

Are you beginning to picture some colors and design elements you want to surround yourself with? Keep in mind that whatever you choose at first doesn't have to stay forever. Like our moods, décor can change.

By creating a Spiritual Oasis with the right ambiance, you will make your prayer life active and immersive. Active prayer is powerful, which is why I want this for you!

CHAPTER FOUR

Supplies

Now that you have your space picked out and some ideas for the ambiance you want to create, you will need a few supplies to set up your Oasis. Anything and everything can be used to create your space.

(I suggest you avoid actual construction because your room needs may change as you grow with the Lord. Planning a construction project takes time, money, and work that might dampen your desire for that prayer room. Best to keep it simple.)

Shower Curtains
They're not just for showers anymore! They come in whimsical and picturesque designs. You can find

shower curtains with woodland and ocean scenes as well as sunrises and night skies. You can also find the most beautiful landscapes and gardens of colorful flowers. Anything you want can most likely be found on a shower curtain.

They usually cost around twenty-five dollars or less and can be hung with expandable curtain rods or tacked to the wall. When you want to change your prayer room décor, you can take that shower curtain into the bathroom and use it for its intended purpose. I love multipurpose things. Waste not, want not, I always say!

Greenery

I like to spruce up my space with some ivy or green garland sprinkled with flowers. You may like an outdoor feel too, and that is easy to create.

Fairy Lights

A garland entwined with battery-powered fairy lights provides a soothing touch of whimsy and allure to your Oasis.

Lighting

Fairy lights are charming, but if you want to read your Bible or write out your prayers, you will need more substantial light. I suggest a lamp that is personal and intimate. You can turn out the other lights in the room and feel alone with God in the glow of the lamplight. If electrical outlets are scarce, many battery-operated lamps are available online.

Seating

Will you sit on the floor? If you are young and flexible enough to do so, you might want a thick floor cushion. If you opt for a chair, I would suggest one with a comfortable cushion. Test it out first. Can you sit there for thirty minutes or more without being distracted by discomfort? (Would you believe that for a couple of years, my Oasis chair was an exercise bike? So even when I was working out my body, I was also developing my prayer muscle!)

Paper or Cards

Make sure to have some notebook paper or index cards handy to write prayer needs and scriptures.

Display Board (and Accessories)

You might need a place to post prayers and reminders, such as a bulletin board or chalkboard. Depending on the board, you will also need chalk, an eraser, pushpins, tape, and/or mounting putty. I like to post scriptures and the names of people I am praying for on a bulletin board or the walls of my Oasis.

Our minds are so prone to wander, and I like to keep the main points in front of me.

Journal

This will enable you to write out your prayers, praise, and love letters to God. Writing in a journal gives you a record to look back through and see how God has answered your prayers and honored your time together.

Chalk

If you are using a chalkboard, remember to have some chalk and an eraser available. You may even want to use colored chalk—there are so many great options available.

Pens

Don't forget the pens! Having to leave your Oasis to find a pen will most likely result in a distraction of some kind. "Mommy, I need a snack!" "Honey, where are the crackers?" When you leave your Oasis, everyone will assume you are available and open for business.

Tissues

When the Holy Spirit comes over you, it can be powerful and joyful, and tears often flow. I always like to be prepared for those special times.

Music

You may have your phone and earbuds, a headset with a micro SD card, or a radio. However you prefer to listen is fine. Music touches the soul in a way other things do not.

It is also a useful tool to shut out other noises around the house. This is your time with the Lord; it's okay to put others' needs on hold for this moment. As long as the children are safe, you can escape here.

Bible

There will be times when a scripture will come to mind, and you will want to find and read it in your Bible. Other times, when you feel overwhelmed and can't find the words to pray, you can open your Bible and begin reading His Word. It's during these times that the revelations are often the most profound.

I keep several versions of the Bible on hand because I have found it helpful to read the text in different ways. Sometimes I need to read a passage in everyday, simple language, and for that reason, I keep *The Message* nearby.

Devotionals

Some of my favorite books are those by authors such as Max Lucado, who write from a biblical worldview. I like books that share stories of everyday people in tough situations along with the faith and prayers that have brought them through. My other favorites are books about the people who wrote famous hymns that tell the message of faith behind the hymns.

I hope this has prompted you to consider items that you already have around your home. You may want to change up your space from time to time to keep things fresh. You could even organize an Oasis group of friends with whom to share prayers and inspiration. When you redecorate your spaces, you could host a prayer room "swap shop." Don't buy what you can borrow! That's good stewardship in action.

But if you are at a loss, check out my Resource List for practical products and inspiration at www.evonn eboggs.com under the "Resources" tab.

CHAPTER FIVE

Inspiration

Inspiration comes from the Holy Spirit, from the Word of God, and from His people. Now, I can suggest devotionals and other resources that may be helpful for the situations you pray about, but the best inspiration comes during our quiet times with the Lord.

The writings that follow come from my times of focus and prayer while designing prayer rooms for women's conferences. When I pray about what to create in a prayer room, God always provides inspiration. Feel free to copy or even tear out these pages to hang on the walls of your Spiritual Oasis. You can also use these excerpts to inspire your own writings.

PURPOSE

We bought one of our sons a beautiful chiminea, which is a freestanding, outdoor fireplace made of clay. It brought many happy moments as it warmed our son and his family and friends with its heat. And so it fulfilled its purpose. Even a beautiful vessel is not fully what it was intended to be until it allows itself to be used. Are you being well used?

The first time I designed a prayer room experience for a conference, it was an act of faith. Somehow, I just knew that I could do it and that God would provide. I had no training in such things, but I had a passion for bringing women into God's presence through beauty. For each conference, I would pray for God's guidance and inspiration; sometimes that inspiration came only a week before the event!

It's times like these when you step out in faith and walk in your purpose. God will not fail to lead you. It takes boldness to live out your purpose. It took me ten years after I knew God wanted me to write this book to begin. It's never too late!

Lord, fill me. Use me for Your purposes, and let me be a comfort to others along the way.

CHOSEN

If you will let Him, God will choose you to change lives. Mother, wife, Sunday school teacher, police officer, counselor, soldier, clerk, IRS agent, nurse, doctor, schoolteacher, X-ray tech ... whatever you are, God chooses *you*. You are His chosen. He has already chosen you to be with Him in eternity. How will you, as God's chosen, reveal Him to others?

> Therefore, as God's chosen ones, holy and dearly loved, put on compassion, kindness, humility, gentleness, and patience... And let the peace of Christ, to which you were also called in one body, rule your hearts. And be thankful. Let the word of Christ dwell richly among you, in all wisdom teaching and admonishing one another through psalms, hymns, and spiritual songs, singing to God with gratitude in your hearts. And whatever you do, in word or in deed, do everything in the name of the Lord Jesus, giving thanks to God the Father through him. (Colossians 3:12, 15–17).

WHY PRAYER?

Do you have a friend who is always there when you need to talk—who listens no matter what time of the day or night? One who understands those parts of you that you aren't brave enough to share with others?

Would you like a friend who understands the tears even before you shed them?

A friend like this does exist. His name is Jesus.

When you are ready to talk to Him, He is always ready to listen. Even if you have ignored Him for years, and even if you have never known Him in a personal way, He is waiting for you.

Bow your head in genuine surrender. Enter this prayer room ready to hear God speak to your heart. Be ready to be "real" in front of Him. He will forgive your mistakes; He understands your failures. He is waiting to hear from you.

You are His beloved daughter.

GOD MOMENTS

One day, I stepped outside, ready to hop in my car and rush off to another errand, when I was stopped in my tracks. There, in front of my house, was the largest, most vibrant rainbow I had ever seen. I was frozen for a moment in awe as memories of God's promises flooded my mind. At that moment, I truly felt His presence, and I didn't want it to end. But, of course, time schedules and to-do lists eventually won out, and the moment passed.

Have you ever had one of those "God moments" in your life?

A field of bluebonnets can make me freeze, and I can almost hear God saying, "This is for you." The fragrance of lavender. The moon when it's full. The artistry of crystal vases. The smile of a child. The sound of a gifted singer lifting praises to our Lord. These are God moments for me.

Where do you find God talking to you? It's so often in nature, isn't it? Enjoy the beauty of His creation. It is a gift to us, His children. He didn't have to make a sunset so beautiful, but for our delight, He painted it so brilliantly.

Take time to appreciate the beauty. Take time to hear Him call. He loves you, precious daughter, and He wants to spend time with you.

AN INVITATION

"Therefore, let us approach the throne of grace with boldness, so that we may receive mercy and find grace to help us in time of need" (Hebrews 4:16).

If we are going to live by grace, we must relate rightly to the God of all grace—namely, by walking in humble dependence. Continual, Spirit-led prayerfulness is the most basic way to express humility and faith in the Lord. How fitting it is then to consider God's invitation to pray at His throne of grace.

The throne to which we are invited is the throne of God, revealed to the Apostle John. " Immediately

I was in the Spirit, and there was a throne in heaven and someone was seated on it" (Revelation 4:2). This exalted King of the universe is the Creator of all things. That is a lot to take in, isn't it? He executes His sovereign will through His limitless power.

"Our Lord and God, you are worthy to receive glory and honor and power, because you have created all things, and by your will they exist and were created" (Revelation 4:11). This is a throne of complete holiness. The angels declare His majesty: "Day and night they never stop, saying, 'Holy, holy, holy, Lord God, the Almighty, who was, who is, and who is to come'" (Revelation 4:8).

For the godless, this will be a throne of judgment. "Then I saw a great white throne and one seated on it... I also saw the dead, the great and the small, standing before the throne, and ... each one was judged according to their works... And anyone whose name was not found written in the book of life was thrown into the lake of fire" (Revelation 20:11–13, 15).

If this throne were only one of power and judgment, we could never approach it with any expectation of blessing. Yet, for those who accept Jesus Christ, this is a throne of grace. "Therefore, let us approach the throne of grace with boldness."

We can approach this throne with spiritual confidence because Jesus is seated there with the Father.

"Then I saw one like a slaughtered lamb standing in the midst of the throne... Worthy is the Lamb who was slaughtered to receive power and riches and wisdom and strength and honor and glory and blessing" (Revelation 5:6, 12)!

The worthy Lamb, who died for our sins, has opened the door to an intimate relationship with our heavenly Father. "For you did not receive a spirit of slavery to fall back into fear. Instead, you received the Spirit of adoption, by whom we cry out, 'Abba, Father!'" (Romans 8:15). "In him we have boldness and confident access through faith in him" (Ephesians 3:12).

Now this throne is to us an altar of prayer for mercy and grace!

Abba, Father, I bow before Your throne, acknowledging You as the sovereign Creator and the holy Judge. Yet, I boldly approach You as my dear, intimate Papa! Although I deserved judgment, now, through Jesus, I humbly request mercy and grace.

FEAR NOT

We see scary things in our world every day. And even though they are indeed scary, we can take comfort that God, our Father, told us that these things would happen before Jesus Christ returns for His children.

In the meantime, we are to be watchful, wise, and faithful.

Fear is paralyzing, but God has prepared us. The command "Fear not" (or "Do not be afraid") is used more than seventy times throughout the Bible.

"Fear not" first appears in Genesis 15:1, the first book of the Bible, and last appears in the final book of Revelation, when John tells us, "When I saw him, I fell at his feet like a dead man. He laid his right hand on me and said, 'Don't be afraid. I am the First and the Last'" (1:17).

To me, this means that God is in control, from beginning to end. Not one thing is happening that He does not see. Not one thing is happening that He cannot protect His children from. Even death has no victory for those who have accepted Jesus Christ as Lord.

So rest, sweet child. Be watchful, be prayerful, but fear not.

THOSE HUSBANDS

God, thank You for the blessing of my husband. He is perfect for me in so many ways, I know.

My husband is not a believer. *Father, please stir his heart and create a hunger for You within. I know that it is Your will that all may know You. I claim this gift for my husband. I pray that You push Your way* *through the sports and the TV and fill his mind with Your ways. If I have to go to church alone while You talk to him, I will. I will honor my commitment to You first, Lord. I trust that You can handle the rest. I love him, and I will honor the promise I made to him in Your presence. I give my husband to You and will stay out of Your way.*

My husband is a godly man. *I thank You, Father, for sending him my way. Little things that he does get on my nerves, but I do love him. He doesn't seem interested in the same things that I enjoy. I go hunting with him just to be with him, but it isn't my favorite activity. And he doesn't want me to talk to him when we are hunting or fishing! But at least we are together. I wish he would enjoy going to a craft fair with me because it brings me such joy. I know men are built differently, but could he just love me like I need to be loved? I pray for change. I stand on the promise of our marriage and pray either for him to change or for me to accept him the way he is.*

My husband is cheating. *Well, I don't know for sure, but I can't handle the hurt if I find out that he is with another person. I am scared that the pain will consume me. Help me, Lord. Give me strength and wisdom. Help me to stand firm and wait on You to work in him. Create in us a new heart. Help us to stand before You strong in our commitment once again. I pray that my husband's heart will be softened and that he will* *look at me again with the joy and love we once had. Help him to turn from evil ways that have invaded his life. Help him to stand strong and righteous.*

This prayer has had a lot of "help" and "give" demands. Let me stop and praise You, Father, for all that You are and all that You do and all that You will do. I will love You all the days of my life and look forward to the reunion with You in heaven. Shower us with Your Holy Spirit, and I will be faithful to spread the blessings to others. Thank You, Lord.

My husband is different. *Oh, boy, is he different! I enjoy comedies; he enjoys war movies. I like to share my day with him; he likes to be left alone. I like to have a clean sink, but he will "get around to it." I like the toilet seat down; he leaves it up. He reads books; I read my tablet. He folds towels in half, and I like them rolled. I like to cuddle—ah, yes, he likes to cuddle too! I like worship music, and he does too. I enjoy church, and he is a man after God's own heart. He is a good provider and a wonderful father. He has a heart for the lost and sparks the same concern in me.*

He is different, but thank You for bringing him into my life. Please teach him to be gentler in his speech and less condemning of my differences. Teach him to appreciate my quirks as I am learning to appreciate his. Bind us together for one purpose: to honor You. As our marriage grows stronger, I pray that we can be a testimony to what You can do with two very different people brought together as one. As we grow closer to You, Lord, I pray that we will grow closer to each other. Let mercy and kindness and joy follow us all the days of our lives.

CHILDREN
Preteens and Teens

Lord, I thank You for the gift of my children. Raising them has been a joyful experience in my life. Now, as they are getting older, I am noticing that their attention is being directed away from You. They would rather spend time on their phones, playing video games, or on dates with the wrong people. I pray that You will direct them back to Your ways and seal them in the ways of the Lord. Watch over them, please. Protect them, Lord. Post mighty angels around their beds—swords drawn and ready to battle the enemy's lies. Let nothing evil take root in their minds. Help them become young men and women who acknowledge and walk with You.

Grandchildren: Birth and Beyond

I look at this woman with the fullness of my grandchild inside her. A beautiful miracle is about to take place. She is changing inside and has a front-row seat to Your miracles. I thank You for this, Lord. I pray You provide wisdom for the medical team and peace for these new parents. Please, Lord, make it possible for them to be aware and joyous each step of the way. I pray that joy will cover the pain as much as possible. Help me be the grandmother that I need to be—the kind who will offer a Jesus story as often as I offer a cookie.

Bullies

I am heartsick about the bullying in my child's school. How dare they insult and threaten this child of God! Lord, help me to love and forgive the bullies too, but I must admit, that is not where my mind first goes! Please send the Holy Spirit to shower peace on the playground.

I rebuke the enemy: No, you cannot *have my child! God knows this child, who has already been given to the Holy One.* Matthew 18:6 says, "But whoever causes one of these little ones who believe in me to fall away—it would be better for him if a heavy millstone were hung around his neck and he were drowned in the depths of the sea."

THE CROWN OF REJOICING

But as for us, brothers and sisters, after we were forced to leave you for a short time (in person, not in heart), we greatly desired and made every effort to return and see you face to face. So we wanted to come to you—even I, Paul, time and again—but Satan hindered us. For who

is our hope or joy or crown of boasting
in the presence of our Lord Jesus at his
coming? Is it not you? Indeed you are our
glory and joy (1 Thessalonians 2:17–20)!

In Philippians, we are told to rejoice always. But honestly, there have been times in my life when I thought that command was a little crazy and impossible. Have you ever thought that too? *How can I rejoice when my prayers weren't answered? How can I rejoice when death is all around and it seems like the enemy is winning?*

The crown of rejoicing that Paul writes about in the first book of Thessalonians teaches us to never give up or give in to the enemy; it teaches us about eternity. "Never will I leave you; never will I forsake you," Jesus says (Hebrews 13:5). And His permanence is reason enough to rejoice!

Just look at all we have! We have been immensely blessed. And the biggest of all our blessings is that God gave His only Son so that by knowing and believing in Him, we can have eternal life. We are daughters of the God of everything. The highest, all-knowing, ever-present King of kings is your Father, and He loves you!

Look at where you are. How did you get here? Did you walk in the door? Shelter is a gift. Your mobility is a gift. Did someone who God has also blessed tell you about this book or give it to you? Then how can you sit here in the comfort of this place and wonder how you are blessed?

This earth and this body of yours that God designed are so miraculously assembled that scientists cannot understand how every piece is crafted. Every tiny insect and every leaf have a purpose; so you too have a higher purpose. Take a walk around. God's gifts to you can be seen everywhere. And if you ask Him, He will show you how to be a blessing to someone else.

So, rejoice, sweet daughter of the Most High King and Lord of lords. He loves you and desires for you to understand pure joy. It's all around you, so raise your hands, lift your voice, and let your heart sing His praises!

Philippians 4:4: "Rejoice in the Lord always. I will say it again: Rejoice!"

What are you thankful for? Take a moment to say, "Thank You, Lord!" Take time to write a note of thanks to Him now, and hang it where you will see it and remember to be grateful.

STRENGTH

You are a warrior who has been given all the protective armor and weapons you need to face the world.

Isaiah 54:17:

"No weapon formed against you will suc-
ceed,
and you will refute any accusation raised
against you in court.
This is the heritage of the Lord's servants,
and their vindication is from me."
This is the Lord's declaration.

Psalm 121:1–2:

I lift my eyes toward the mountains.
Where will my help come from?
My help comes from the Lord,
the Maker of heaven and earth.

We sometimes forget this significant fact:

Your strength comes from the Lord. When you feel weak, He is strong. When you think you cannot bear another problem, He is strong. When grief comes into your life, and you feel you cannot go on, He is strong. No matter what may come your way, you can be strong by leaning on God. He is able to give you whatever strength you may need. He will never leave His daughter helpless.

THE IMPERISHABLE CROWN

"Don't you know that the runners in a stadium all race, but only one receives the prize? Run in such a way to win the prize. Now everyone who competes exercises self-control in everything. They do it to receive a perishable crown, but we an imperishable crown" (1 Corinthians 9:24–25).

Faithful endurance wins the imperishable crown. To keep going when the enemy is at your heels—to keep your eyes focused on Christ when they are full of tears: this is endurance.

Father, be with Your daughter right now. Dry her tears, mend her heart, and infuse her with the peace of the Holy Spirit. Show her the beauty of Your presence, and show her how strong she can be with Your help. In Jesus' name, I pray. Amen.

What will you lay down to gain the crown of endurance? Soldiers and athletes know that endurance comes through training. The training we're talking about here involves serious spiritual strength. Spiritual battles can't be fought with flesh and blood; these battles must be fought with the knowledge and power of the Holy Spirit. All you need to overcome this world can be learned at the feet of Jesus.

Lay down the remote control—pick up the Word of God.

Lay down gossip—pick up words that uplift others.

Lay down hopelessness—pick up the acceptance of your identity as God's precious child. You are loved beyond measure. This is love that is hard for us to understand because it is so perfect and so deep and so true and so permanent.

Lay down the immorality of the world—pick up a sword, slay the enemy, and pray that your armor will be strengthened against all of Satan's lies. Gain strength to live in God's true best for you.

Lay down regrets—pick up a plan. The past cannot be redone. A river's water may flow this way, but only once, and then it's gone. So it is with your life. Let your past encourage you to make a plan to avoid making that mistake again. Learn what you can from it, and then move on.

What is in your life right now that is not of God? What is that one thing that you can't seem to resist and causes you to stumble? Write it down on a piece of paper and post it on the wall. Whenever you are tempted by it, go to this paper and draw a big X on it. You may eventually draw so many Xs that you can't see the word, and that's about the time when you'll realize it's not important to you anymore.

CHAPTER SIX

Surrender

"**G**oing a little farther, he fell facedown and prayed, 'My Father, if it is possible, let this cup pass from me. Yet not as I will, but as you will'" (Matthew 26:39).

"And he said, '*Abba*, Father! All things are possible for you. Take this cup away from me. Nevertheless, not what I will, but what you will'" (Mark 14:36).

Surrender is a beautiful word and practice that should be a part of our love language. In my marriage, I would surrender eating garlic before going to bed if only my spouse did the same! Seriously though, many acts of love can be offered to one another daily as we surrender our own wants and comforts for those of others.

But with God, surrender is all-encompassing. Surrender influences my every decision ... or it should. Sometimes I get scared that God's best for me is something I don't want to do. If I turn away from His best for me, the results can be sad and even disastrous. However, if I raise my hands in the air—"I surrender!"—and give Him everything, the results can only be perfect.

Have you ever done a trust fall? This is when you stand with a person (or persons) at your back and you fall backward with the expectation that they will catch you. They always do, but—boy, is that a hard thing to do! It takes a lot of trust in that person. What if they look away or get distracted? *Boom!* You land flat on your back! But that never happens. They always catch you, and another lesson in trust is accomplished.

Now that you are in your Spiritual Oasis, you can practice surrender. For when we pray, we surrender our will and our plans. We leave the outcome to the only One who can make it perfect. Remember, the outcome may not *perfectly* line up with your plan. But you have to trust that even if the answer is on a different schedule or totally different than what you thought you wanted, you still surrender your will to His for the situation. In time, you will see how perfect His plan is.

So, treasured child of God, turn on some praise music, dance in the Spirit, and raise your hands in holy surrender!

CHAPTER SEVEN

Plan of Salvation

To be saved, we have to understand that we need saving. I thought for years that I was a "good person" who would certainly go to heaven someday. I knew that I didn't believe everything in the Bible, but is all that really necessary? Well, as it turns out, it is.

I read Romans 3:23 and found out that "all have sinned and fall short of the glory of God." *What? I'm not sin-free? My good isn't good enough?*

We all sin. From the gossip over brunch to the hateful thoughts while driving in traffic to the rejection of God's Word—it's all sin, and none of it is less offensive than the other.

Sin is a detour away from God; it is deciding that you know better. God is perfectly good, and if He let sin into His Kingdom, it wouldn't be perfect any-more, would it? It would be dirtied by the sin of the world. God's plan to get all of us into the Kingdom was to provide a covering for our sin. That covering was the blood of His Son, Jesus Christ.

Jesus came into the world as God's only Son, born of a virgin. When Jesus surrendered His life on the cross so that His blood would be shed to cover our sins, it was the greatest act of love ever witnessed. When I read about that in the Bible, its reality hit me, and everything changed.

Christmas became different. It was no longer about wrapped gifts and Santa Claus. It was about a depth of love that I had never known. It was a depth of love that I could never repay nor ignore. Jesus is the key to the Kingdom of God and eternal life.

Jesus died to cover all our sins. We still sin; no one is perfect. But because of Jesus, we can admit our sin and receive forgiveness, if we truly want to turn away from that sin. By that, I mean that I can't sin on Monday, ask for forgiveness, and then intentionally commit the same sin on Tuesday. We must repent, which means being truly sorry for the sin, and commit to turn away from it. Then forgiveness is complete.

The doors of heaven are open wide, and our eternal life is secured.

Romans 10:17 says, "So faith comes from what is heard, and what is heard comes through the message about Christ." Consider the following verses as you read them (out loud) in sequence (emphases mine):

Romans 3:23: "**For all have sinned** and fall short of the glory of God."

Romans 6:23: "**For the wages of sin is death** [hell], but the gift of God is eternal life in Christ Jesus our Lord."

John 3:3: "Jesus replied, 'Truly I tell you, **unless someone is born again, he cannot see the kingdom of God.**'"

Now ask yourself, "Why did Jesus come to die?"

John 14:6: "Jesus told him, '**I am the way**, the truth, and the life. No one comes to the Father except through Me.'"

Romans 10:9–11: "**If you confess with your mouth**, 'Jesus is Lord,' and **believe in your heart** that God raised him from the dead, **you will be saved.** One believes with the heart, resulting in righteousness, and one confesses with the mouth, resulting in salvation. For the Scripture says, Everyone who believes on him will not be put to shame."

2 Corinthians 5:15: "And he died for all so that those who live should **no longer live for themselves**, but for the one who died for them and was raised."

Revelation 3:20: "See! **I stand at the door and knock**. If anyone hears my voice and opens the door, I will come in to him and eat with him, and he with me."

Acknowledgments

It was a chance encounter, some might say, that led me to Brenda Haire at a women's conference I was attending for the first time at Alto Frio Baptist Camp and Conference Center. Brenda, you have been an encourager, teacher, and prayer partner. You walked into the prayer experience I had created, and tears began to flow. I knew at that moment that our meeting was not by chance but rather by God's design. Without you, I would still be saying, "I should write a book about that someday." "Someday" has arrived.

Karen Cunningham, who provided much-needed proofreads over the years: I have come to respect and appreciate your detail-orientated nature, and I treasure your friendship.

Thank you to the many friends and family whose prayers have sustained me during these years of discovering how to design visually moving prayer experiences.

And thanks to the many volunteers who came alongside to help us create that apple tree, build walls for the garden setting, and turn windows into replicas of stained-glass art. You all provided the hands to make the vision work, and I am so thankful. I hope you know that you were the answer to many prayers. I have seen God at work through your efforts: Campers on Mission (COM), Servants on Wheels Ever Ready (SOWER), and Roving Volunteers in Christ's Service (RVICS).

Thank you to the North American Mission Board (NAMB) of the Southern Baptist Convention for their Vision Center. The way it displayed prayer needs was outstanding and life-changing. That experience opened my mind to creative ways of displaying reality so that prayer needs may be realized.

For the picture of that beautiful sunset on the cover, I give thanks to Kate Pline. You came around at just the right time and reminded me of seeds planted many years ago. I am excited to see what God has for the future.

To my wonderful editor, Dara Powers Parker, who gave me the confidence to keep writing: You made the process less scary. I believe God led me to you because

your ideas seemed to mesh with my vision effortlessly.
"Thank you" is too small a sentiment.

About the Author

Who am I? Just a Texas girl with big dreams and a heart full of hope. As a child, I envisioned myself a nurse, only to later change course after an unpleasant encounter with blood. Then I fancied myself a teacher, practicing writing my name on my grandma's blackboard: "Mrs. _____ (insert last name of whichever boy I admired at the time)."

At the age of fourteen, I became a wife and mother, embracing a dream I didn't fully understand yet. That marriage didn't last, but my baby girl filled my life with unexpected joys and challenges. I nursed her through scraped knees and flu seasons and taught her about the many possibilities of life. To provide for us, I joined the U.S. Army, beginning a journey that would shape both our lives in ways I never anticipated.

I learned to put others first: my God, my daughter, and my country came before everything else.

I met my husband while on active duty in St. Louis, Missouri, and we blended my daughter and his sons into a sweet and busy family. With a twenty-one-year army career, a master's in Christian education from New Orleans Baptist Theological Seminary, along with a heart for missions and children's ministry, I found my calling in serving others. My life has been a tapestry of diverse roles: soldier, mother, Girl Scout leader/trainer, missionary, grandmother of nine, and great-grandmother of one and a half. My husband and I just celebrated our thirty-second anniversary. Our family now stretches across the United States, from Maine south to Kentucky and west to Oregon, and so I make each moment of connection intentional.

In my thirties, I had finally surrendered my life to God, and He began to guide me through every twist and turn. I became a student, learning to embrace His grace and purpose. I now find great joy in helping others heal their emotional scars and discover God's love and provisions through prayer. While I'm not always perfect at prayer myself, writing prayers and exploring God's ways keeps me grounded in faith.

If you're seeking someone to create a meaningful prayer experience for you or need guidance in setting up your own, I would be delighted to assist. Join me in exploring the depths of God's love and discovering the joy of intentional connection.

Connect at evonneboggs.com.

Work with Evonne

Any time spent in prayer is fruitful.

But I longed for something more in my prayer life.

I have been designing prayer experiences—prayer rooms and prayer stations—for women's conferences for more than 15 years. Each experience is a visual representation of the conference theme, and so each one is different. God has always provided the inspiration in His perfect timing.

Whatever your theme, I would love to work with you to create a prayer experience that draws your participants into transformational prayer. I can provide complete prayer room designs or consult with you to create your own. I want to help you accomplish what God is calling you to do.

- Women's Conferences

- Marriage Conferences

- Focused Prayer Experiences in Your Church

- Workshops on Developing a Spiritual Oasis in Your Home

Evonne Boggs
Prayer Experience
770-826-5291
evonneboggs@yahoo.com

Endnotes

1. * Graham, Ron. "Places People Prayed: A Simple List from the Bible." SimplyBible.com . 2018. https://www.simplybible.com/f40w-bilis-places-people-prayed.htm.

2. Christopher Beatty, *Holy Ground*, in *Baptist Hymnal* (Nashville: LifeWay Worship, 2008), 71.